I am Bear Watcher

Watching Bear Watching

Me

By Jay North

When I was just a boy, perhaps six or seven years of age I was camped with a few friends in Sequoia National Park in California. My Father would take a group of boys up into the high country all over California every year until my late teens. Sequoia is an amazing place and I highly recommend it for outdoor enthusiasts. Even today at age seventy it is a favorite pick for week long get a-ways.

Back to my first experience of the bear, up in these massive and majestic Sequoia trees. We were camped in a prepared campsite run by the National Forest. Early our first morning, after a long drive up the long twisty road at night - we, the other boys and my dad, slept in until eight in the morning. Dad woke us, "Time for breakfast" - which meant to my dad oatmeal. A family of nice size or should I say huge California Bruins (bears) showed up for breakfast as well, only they wanted what was left over in the trash cans. One unwise camper walked over to these beasts and started to tease with them. I was naive but I somehow knew this was a bad idea. My father got out his eight millimeter movie camera and filmed what turned out to be a disaster. The hump back daddy of a bear swatted the man's leg and broke it at the ankle.

Meanwhile, an Indian man, now referred to Native or Native American, came over to our site, he sat at the picnic table and he said to me, "You are a 'bear watcher', brave and wise." I noticed your marvel at these great creatures and you did not flinch a muscle. While the rest of the camp was screaming 'BEAR', you stayed put and just observed that fool getting his leg broken. My boy I will tell you this, my people have great respect for the animals of the forest and the Great Bear is our brother. They are to be respected, never killed, and always, they are always keen when humans are present. These bears today meant no harm to anyone. The taunting by that ignorant person may cost the Great Bear his life—as the forestry managers will consider him a danger and take his life from him." That made me very sad to hear.

"Young lad, this is a sad and a good day. You witnessed a massive and wondrous brother bear, you observed him, respected him and appreciated his beauty. My name is 'Bear Watcher', I am the bear, I am the bear watcher. I would name you 'Bear Watcher Many Bears' out of respect for you diligence to sit quietly and observe. You will experience many more bears in your life. I would advice, when you are of age to carry *bear medicine with you wherever you go and especially into the woods," and he departed.

Dad came back to camp, "Who was that," he asked, referring to my adviser.
"That was an Indian, pop, his name is 'Bear Watcher' and so is mine."
"Come on lets get you set up to go catch some trout," dad said.
"Okay," I replied, "but I am going to feed them to the bears."
 "You will do no such thing," said pop.

Half of a lifetime later and living in the majestic silver state - Montana, I would have four encounters with the great bear, only these were the Grizzly Bear,

and oh my they are truly huge and massively beautiful, oh, and dangerous.

Some Call Me Bear Watcher

Some Others Call Me Bear People

Does Not Mater Much To Me

I Know Who I Am

I Am Bear Watcher

Watching ME

Pammy don't run

My(our) first encounter with this incredibly beautiful
beast (Grizzly Bear) in Montana was on the west-side
of the great divide not far from our home. My bride
and I were scouting for elk up above Big Fork Montana, up in the foothills. We hiked around two miles
up and hit a major incline. "This is so beautiful," my
wife said, "lets keep going." We did about another
two hundred yards and there it was. Sitting on his
rump devouring Huckleberries.
"Oh dear," Pammy said.
"Just stay still," I said, "don't run." This massive Griz
looked at me looked at here, back at me. Pammy
spooked and ran down hill.
I said, "Mr. Bear, if you even think about chasing her
I will have to shoot you, please don't make me do
that."
Mr. Griz, as though he was laughing, turned and
walked further up hill. No we did not score an Elk,
nor a Griz.

This Ground Bear Watcher

Walks Upon

Is Sacred Ground

Tred Upon Her Her

With Ease

Damn it, Les - you should know better

My next encounter would be with a new-found friend
in Montana—he was born and raised in the silver
state and should have known better. Les and I became
fly fishing buddies, and we fished together often both
on the west side of the great divide and over east under the incredibly beautiful massive peaks of Glacier
National Park.

This day we chose the west side near the town of
Whitefish and fly fished our way up stream six miles
into the Whitefish river country. This is as close to
wild back woods as anyone can get. Packed full of
wild East Slope Cutthroat.** Not exactly an easy
stroll, as this is a rocky uneven base.
"Les," I said, "I think we better think about heading
out of here, its two in the afternoon and we have a
hell of a walk out." Without even another word spo-
ken - there he was.
"Oh dang, lets wait him out for a few minutes and see
what he thinks of the situation."
He began to charge, Les began to run. "Les I shouted,
don't run, don't run."
Les went down and smashed his right knee on a rock.
"Les, you are going to need help getting out of here
and that means I have to walk out and get help, stay
alive my friend I will be back for you."
Griz sat watching and listening.
I said, "Mr Griz, we got a situation here and I need
you to behave. My friend is hurt, he needs medical as-
sistance and soon - now you scoot off, leave him
alone and I will just back out of here."

I began a six mile walk out, it was dark, it was cold, and I was getting pooped. Motivated by my friends dis-stress I knew I had to keep going. Five hours later I found my old white ford pick up and let out a cry - "Thank goodness." I drove down to the town of Whitefish, went to the police station and told of what happened. The Chief of police came back to the office, he made the decision to wait for forestry and pursue the treacherous trek up stream in the morning. "But sir, my friend is injured, has no blanket nor food. Plus," I continued, "he could become the bears dinner."

He replied, "We have no choice, its pitch black out there with no moon, even if we send a helicopter we won't see him." He advised me to get as comfortable as I could get some rest and be prepared to head up river in the early am. I reached out to Les (in spirit) and great bear in my mind. I wanted to communicate to both, "Everything is okay."

Early AM; This hike up river is no walk in the park, not bad when one is concentrated on fishing, but when in a hurry, oh my it is tough at the very least. A helicopter overhead radioed to law enforcement that they had Less spotted, they would hold their position until we got to him. Les was more or less in one piece - that is to say no body parts had been eaten. We were just two hundred yards off Mr Bear. "I am watching you watching us - thank you for not eating my friend," I said when we arrived to Less's side. Les was air lifted out and we, Law Enforcement and Forestry, walked out again the whole six miles - tailed by the Griz.

I am Bear Watcher
I Share This Ground
With Many Kinds

Truth be told I love fly fishing as much as I love life itself

In my late 40's I decided to become a fly fishing guide. I had a man call from San Francisco and ask about week-long fly fishing in Montana. We agreed on a date and he arrived sweating and chomping at the hook, so to speak, to get out and catch a massive brown trout - a prize anywhere in the lower 48. He slapped $500.00 cash on the dining room table.
I asked, "Whats that for?"
"I want a monster I can mount," he replied.
"Sir, I'll take that five hundred, but I will not guarantee you a six incher."

"Listen my friend, relax, settle down," I pleaded.
"You are going to be in fly fishing heaven for a week and I will put you over fish, but you won't catch one until you settle down. We will fish the east side of the divide and the west, I will put you over fish in lakes, streams and tiny creeks, but unless you take a breather I will take you back to the airport."
He did settle down and yes, he caught his wall mount.

We were headed back west on highway 2 to take him back to his gear and fly home. Heading out of the east side I thought I should give him an opportunity at these beautiful West Slope Cutthroats.** I stopped at Midvale Creek and said, "Lets see if they are in the neighborhood." This is just below an old train grain spill, where bears like to eat the fermented corn and get drunk. Not a minute after getting out of the truck, she (griz) comes running down from the train tracks,

stops just across the creek from our position. She looks at my client, looks at me and I said out loud, "Oh lord, please have her eat me, because if she eats him, his family will sure sue the hell out of me."
She looks at me, looks at him, glances up hill to her cubs, and shoots back up the hill.
My client peed his pants I said, "Now that is a Montana experience."

Bear Watcher Watching Me
I am Watching Him
We Bear Watchers
Watch Each Other

Back to California 1998, my bride had passed away

I would revisit the eastern and western streams and lakes by my self for many years to come - if I don't die of grief that is.

It had been more than just a few years since Pammy's passing. I was lonely and figured a dog would be nice to have along on my fly fishing trips - hence Walter came into my life - a long story in its self. Walter would be my side by side fly fishing companion for 12.5 years. This is just one experience among hundreds we had together.

We had been fishing the Eastern Sierra for about two weeks and soon it would be time to head home and get my butt back to work. We were camped together on Lee Vinning Creek and I said, "Walter my boy, this has been a great trip but me we gotta head home in the morning." He didn't even raise his head as he thought I was kidding, I am quite sure. Walter was a very expressive boy, and independent. We were fishing off the bank of the Lee Vinning river and there he was - not four yards off our trail, a huge Bruin. Walter was sitting right at my feet. I spun my fly reel to gain line for a cast and boom right in the river - the bear, I did not see but WALTER certainly did, jumped into the creek. "BEAR," I screamed, which it not a normal action for me. The bear turned to watch us. "Walter-the dog lets just back out of here," and we did. We arrived at the motor home, got in the captains seats and watched the old boy walk up stream, knock the trash can over and eat the fish guts. ERG gee, "Walter you could have said something."

Next morning we walked up stream, hit a big hole
and caught really nice size rainbow, all the while
watching the bear watching us. Time to head home.

This Is The Place
Of
Original Bear Watching
We Come From
Right Here
Watching the Bear

Slowing down a bit

I am older now and I don't get out as much as I used to, both Pammy and Walty are gone, but I try to manage walks the best I can, with a few health issues and semi-disabled, I still dream of the illusive trout and being healthy enough to go again, and I did.
Traveling with the Bears

In the year 2014; I scored a rather substantial assignment, and being a foot-loose-fancy-free-gypsy-type-a-guy - I decided it would be best to do this assignment on the road. Perfect! So, I loaded up the abode on wheels (the RV) and hit the road. I would stop at the most interesting places I could find in America, and visited thirty states. I would check in with my client once or twice a week, drive days and work nights in the abode. Had plenty, I mean plenty of coffee on hand and wrote like a bear turned lose - speed and accuracy was my credo, and where I folded up, editors would certainly fix up. I pulled out of California, hit the most interesting parts of the Southwest, then Midwest, down to the deep south, drove up the coast to New York City, up to Maine, back down to Arkansas, the left turn up to Montana. I love the phrase; "Montana I'll Be Back," then over to Wyoming, Idaho, Washington, down to Oregon, left to Utah and back down to Arizona. I always like to tell people I fly fished 29 states illegally. I got back to California late November at two in the morning - got out of the abode at Malibu, took a deep breath and said to my self, "I am home," Thank God all mighty I am home. Oh, but wait, there is more; these are stories of bear sightings and communion with Nature. Well, I saw brother bear in every state except Florida.

There Is No Other Place To
Watch Bear
We are Unique
Bear Watchers

One lovely incident in Washington up in the Cas-
cades, a magical morning, heavy fog, a brisk morning, and plenty of wild-life. I was up somewhere mid-
state WA. Not far from Canada but not close enough
to hear the word 'about' like a Sargent drill. Haa! This
looks nice, turn right here, go about 2 miles, pull over
and camp for the night - a long night of pounding the
keyboard.

Out at 6:00 am for a deep breath in the moist woods, I
decided a short walk would be in order. Reached into
the abode grabbed my jacket and a sandwich from last
night - off I was on an magnificent morning stroll
among the conifers, ferns and Morel Mushrooms. I
was walking slowly and quietly while grazing on the
Shrooms.

Almost like magic, there they are mom and two babes
making there way down a rock and slippery face on
the side of the mountain. I gotta say; this took my
breath away - a magical morning of fresh doe, tasty
shrooms and three cinnamon bear. The babies were so
dam cute I wanted to take them home with me. I got
to stand in silence for about 20 minutes watching the
threesome traversing their way to solid flat ground.
Mom stiffed me and push the children to dense Huck-
leberry brush. I only had one more glimpse before
they blended in and left my sight. I bent down on my
knee and crying; "Thank you spirit, thank you for this
day."

I said it before and say it again

There is nothing but Nature

Watching the Bear Watching Me

Along came love-- for a minute

I befriended a lovely little gal here in Ojai CA, I asked her if she would come for a walk with me and possibly meet the Little People also known as The Earth People up in the woods above the town. She replied, "I would love to."

We packed a lunch and made out on a drive just eight miles out of town. This is a short, but truly amazing walk. She seemed to know to stay quiet instinctively. She watched for signs of the little people in silence and with reverence. We washed our faces in the stream, saw a few tiny trout, and continued our walk up hill.

"Jay," ever so quietly she said, "look, a bear."
"Oh my, she is a beauty," I commented. She was a cinnamon, slightly starving after a major fire, and eating tall dry bear grass. My lady friend asked," Are we safe?"
I replied, "Bears never bother me, I don't bother them and neither do you."
She, the bear, sniffed us out and took off. "Oh my this is a good day," I thought.

"I Am Bear Watcher Many Bears Is My Name"

* Bear Medicine, used in sacred ceremony and also carried as a good luck charm.

** East and West Slope Cutthroat Trout are distinctly different, East slope trout have practically no color, while west slope are lite like gold and both have an obvious red line (cut) under their jaw gills.

But Still A Bear Watcher
In Nature

"Bears are not companions of men, but chil-

dren of God." — Charles Muir

24

"Bears not only make the habitat rich, but they also enrich us just by being." — Linda Jo Hunter

Jay North Other Books

Open Spaces: My Life With Leonard J. Mountain Chief
Return To Open Spaces- The Final Chapter
Emergence Of The Rainbow Tribe
Spirit Filled Prayers and Affirmations: The Process
Thoughts Without Thinking
The Gift of Touch -Massage and Energy Healing
Miracles in the Kitchen
Create the Life You Have Always Dreamt About
Walter's Big Adventure
Getting Started in Organic Gardening
The Windowsill Organic Gardener
How to Cure Cancer Naturally
And many others…
Future books to come also by Jay North
Many Roads Traveled, true story of Jay North's life- a work in progress
What Really Happened The True Story of The Sixties
accounting of Black & White TV, Tragedy and Overcoming
Fleeing Russia, the true story of my grandfather
In Service of Her God, Jays deceased wife Pamela Victoria North's
 life of service-the unfamed 1st St. Theresa
Perhaps Walter's Big Adventure II
The Land of Oshkosh; Tiny Blue Blob and Baby Red Lou Arrive

———————————

Jays books found at www.OneGlobePress.com